FITNESS
FOR FUN!

By Dana Meachen Rau

Content Adviser: Phil Haberstro, Executive Director, National Association for Health and Fitness, Buffalo, N.Y.
Reading Adviser: Susan Kesselring, M.A., Literacy Educator, Rosemount-Apple Valley-Eagan (Minnesota) School District

Compass Point Books ✦ Minneapolis, Minnesota

Compass Point Books
151 Good Counsel Drive
P.O. Box 669
Mankato, MN 56002-0669

 This book was manufactured with paper containing at least 10 percent post-consumer waste.

Photographs ©: Kelly Redinger/Design Pics/Corbis, front cover (left); Karon Dubke/Capstone Press, front, back cover (sneakers), 19, 20 (top, middle) 21, (all); Jacek Chabraszewski/Shutterstock, 4; Galina Barskaya/Shutterstock, 5; Stock Connection USA/Newscom, 6; HIP/Art Resource, N.Y., 7, 42 (middle); Sebastian Kaulitzki/Shutterstock, 8, 9; Michael D. Brown/Shutterstock, 11; Diego Cervo/Shutterstock, 12; Noam Armonn/Shutterstock, 13, 47; Lisa F. Young/Shutterstock, 14; Michael DeLeon/iStockphoto, 15; Sean Nel/Shutterstock, 16; Darren Green/Shutterstock, 17; Andrjuss/Shutterstock, 18; Andrey Armyagov/Shutterstock, 20 (bottom); Jeff Greenberg/Alamy, 23; Eric Delmar/iStockphoto, 23 (bottom); aceshot1/Shutterstock, 24; Stephen Mallon/Photonica/Getty Images, 25; Marcus Clackson/Photonica/Getty Images, 27; David Young-Wolff/PhotoEdit, 28, 29; Tony Freeman/PhotoEdit, 30; Victoria Graca/Shutterstock, 32; Olga Semicheva/Shutterstock, 33 (top); Kirk Winslow/iStockphoto, 33 (bottom); Steve Lovegrove/iStockphoto, 34; clu/iStockphoto, 35; D. Clarke Evans/© 2008 NBAE/ NBAE via Getty Images, 36; Vasiliki Varvaki/iStockphoto, 37; Dana Meachen Rau, 39; Josef Philipp/iStockphoto, 40; Stephen Bonk/Shutterstock, 41; The Bridgeman Art Library/Getty Images, 42 (left); ABACAUSA.com/APEGA/Newscom, 42 (right); Lyndon Baines Johnson Library, 43 (left); Claudio Onorati/AFP/Newscom, 43 (middle); Masakazu Watanabe/AFLO Sport/Newscom, 43 (right); Monkia Graff/UPI/Newscom, 44 (left); Douglas McCarthy/Mary Evans Picture Library, 44 (right); Linda Bucklin/Shutterstock, 45.

Editor: Brenda Haugen
Page Production: Ashlee Suker
Photo Researcher: Marcie Spence
Art Director: LuAnn Ascheman-Adams
Creative Director: Joe Ewest
Editorial Director: Nick Healy
Managing Editor: Catherine Neitge

Library of Congress Cataloging-in-Publication Data
Rau, Dana Meachen, 1971–
   Fitness for fun! / by Dana Meachen Rau.
      p. cm. — (For Fun!: Sports)
   Includes index.
   ISBN 978-0-7565-4031-9 (library binding)
1. Exercise—Juvenile literature. I. Title.
   GV461.3.R38 2009
   613.7'042—dc22   2008037570

Visit Compass Point Books on the Internet at www.compasspointbooks.com
or e-mail your request to custserv@compasspointbooks.com

Table of Contents

Note: In this book, there are two kinds of vocabulary words. Fitness Words to Know are words specific to fitness. They are defined on page 46. Other Words to Know are helpful words that are not related only to fitness. They are defined on page 47.

Feeling Fit

Think of a machine that can do your homework, clean up your room, and get you to the bus on time. Imagine that the machine can run fast, climb high, and ride a bike. It can think, read, and even tell jokes.

That machine is you! Your body has many parts that work together. You have to take care of this special machine.

Fitness is being well and healthy. You need physical activity to be fit. Physical activity will help you live longer and fight diseases. It will

Get Happy

When you are physically active, your body makes endorphins. These chemicals in your brain are known to make you happy. So stay active to be as happy as you can be.

strengthen your bones and muscles and help your brain think clearly. It will help you sleep well at night and feel good during the day.

Start with a fitness goal. Maybe your goal can be to run a mile without stopping. Maybe you want to cross the monkey bars without falling. Maybe you want to be able to touch your nose to your knees. With regular physical activity, you can reach your goal and be fit.

Fit to Survive

More than 10,000 years ago, people had to be fit to survive. They lived by hunting (right) and needed to travel long distances to find food. They explored new lands on foot. When people started to settle down and farm, their bodies had to be strong to plow the soil and harvest crops.

As more people settled closer together, civilizations grew. They took over other lands by going to war. People had to be fit to enter battle.

People in history also stayed fit for fun and competition. The ancient Greeks (right) started the Olympic Games in 776 B.C. In Greece, only men were allowed to compete in events such as running, wrestling, chariot races, and discus throwing.

As time went on, physical education developed as people taught others ways to be fit. People began to realize that physical activity helped prevent diseases. They created specific exercises to strengthen the heart or to help people who were sick get stronger after an illness.

Governments even became involved in keeping their citizens fit. In the United States, presidents have developed programs to help kids and adults set healthy activity goals.

The Modern Olympics

The modern Olympics started in 1896. Now the Olympic Games are held in both summer and winter every four years. Athletes come from all over the world to compete to see who are the best at their sports.

Special Delivery!

Inside, your body is like a city, filled with streets that lead to every part. These pathways through your body are part of your circulatory system (right). The circulatory system is made up of your heart, the pathways called vessels, and the blood that travels through them.

Your body also takes in and lets out air. This is your respiratory system. Your lungs are the main organs of this system. They take oxygen out of the air. Oxygen is the part of air your body needs to function.

These systems work together to deliver oxygen and other nutrients to all parts of your body. First, you breathe air into your lungs. Your lungs take the oxygen out of the air. Your heart pumps blood into your lungs (right) to pick up this oxygen. The blood with oxygen now goes back into the heart. The heart pumps this blood out through vessels that travel to all parts of your body. The blood comes back to the heart through other vessels. And the process starts all over again.

When you are active, your muscles need more blood. So your breathing gets quicker and your heart beats faster. Exercise makes your heart and lungs stronger.

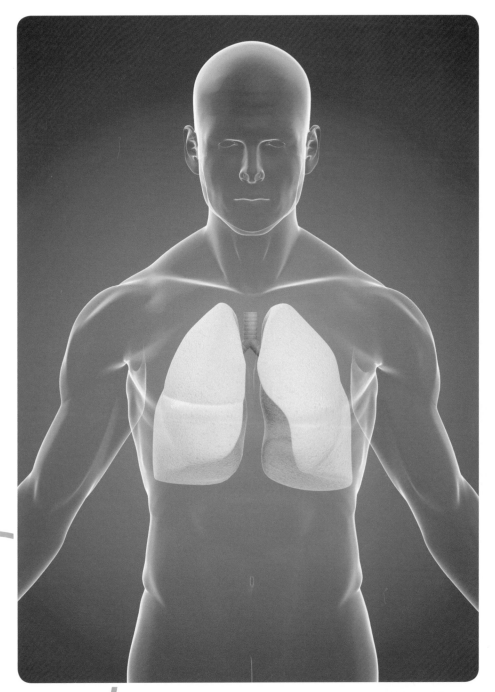

Mighty Muscles

You use muscles to move. The muscles in your arms help you climb. The muscles in your legs help you walk. The muscles in your face help you look surprised.

Some muscles, such as your heart, are always working without you having to think about it. But you decide to use skeletal muscles, the ones attached to your bones. If you want to pick up a pencil, you have to think about it first. Your brain then sends a message to your muscles to make your fingers move.

At the Joint

A joint is where two bones meet and move. Your jaw, knees, shoulders, and wrists are some of your joints.

When you want to move, the muscles pull the bone where it needs to go. Muscles stretch to get longer and contract to get shorter.

You may find your legs ache after you run. Or your arms ache after you lift something heavy. When you are active, more blood flows to your muscles. They work much harder than when they are at rest. If they are not strong enough to do what you ask them to do, they may feel sore. But regular physical activity can help make your muscles stronger.

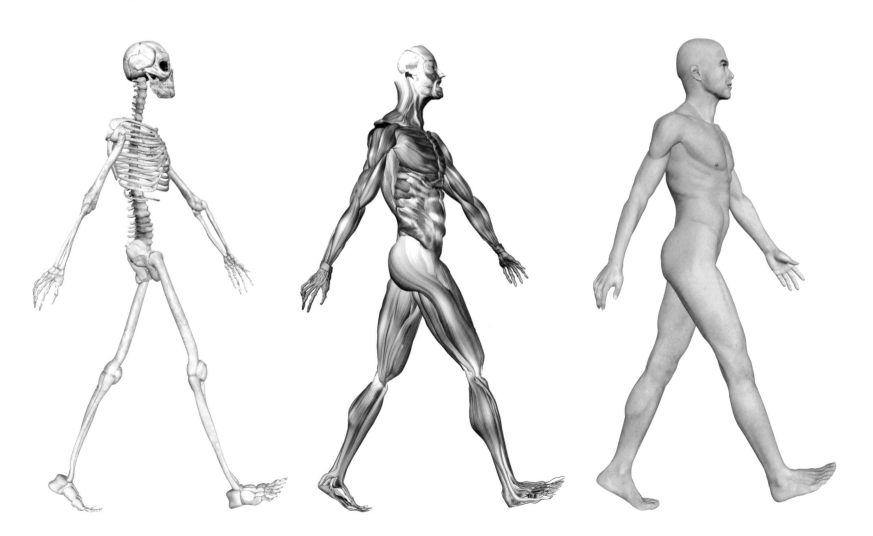

Aerobic

The three types of fitness activities are aerobic, strength, and flexibility. Aerobic activities strengthen your heart so it can better deliver oxygen and nutrients to your body.

Aerobic activities get your heart pumping. Play a game of tag, jump rope, or start a soccer match. Bike-riding, swimming, running, basketball, tennis, and hockey also strengthen your heart.

Be sure you get at least 60 minutes of physical activity each day. That can include helping with household chores, walking, or any of the other aerobic activities already listed. Just get moving!

Strength

Strength exercises focus on making individual muscles or muscle groups stronger. When you have strong muscles, you are better able to perform your favorite activities and household chores.

You can do a lot of strength exercises right on the playground. Crossing the monkey bars works your arm muscles. Climbing a ladder works both your arms and legs.

You can do some strength exercises on the floor. For a sit-up, lie on your back with bent legs and curl your chest toward your knees. For a push-up, lie facedown, line your hands with your shoulders, and push your body up off the floor, using your knees or toes for support.

With strength exercises, you repeat the same exercise over and over. Each try is a repetition, or "rep." You let your muscles relax between sets of reps. Each day you can increase your number of reps as your muscles get stronger. Fifteen reps is a good goal for any strength exercise.

Sit-up

Weight Training

When you get older, you might use weights to do strength exercises. But lifting too much weight can strain or tear your muscles. It's better to do more reps with a light weight than just a few lifts with a heavy weight. Before you start lifting weights, it's a good idea to talk to your physical education teacher about your goals and to learn the proper techniques.

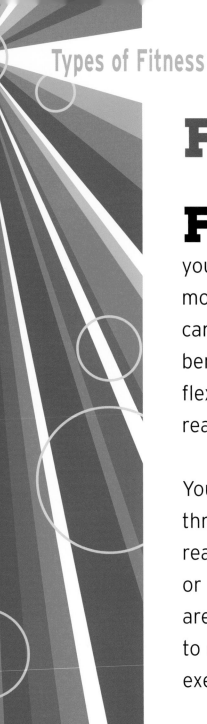

Flexibility

Flexibility is the ability of your muscles and joints to move easily. People who can touch their toes without bending their knees are more flexible than those who can't reach their toes.

You can increase your flexibility through stretching. Every time you reach to get a book off a high shelf or lean over to tie your shoe, you are stretching. Stretching is great to do before aerobic or strength exercises. But stretching shouldn't be used as a warm-up. See page 22 for tips on how to properly warm up your muscles.

You can stretch your neck by moving your head from side to side. Then do a butterfly stretch. Sit on the floor with the bottom of your feet together and hold your ankles, pressing your legs down. To stretch your whole body, stand and reach up with your arms.

Stretching and other flexibility exercises shouldn't hurt. Stretch until you feel tension, or a slight pull, in your muscles. Hold the stretch for 10 to 30 seconds. Remember

to ease into your stretch and to ease out of your stretch. Don't bounce or bob, which can damage your muscles.

Besides stretches, some other exercises help your flexibility. Dancing, martial arts, gymnastics, and yoga (below) all help your muscles and joints move more freely.

Your Body Fuel

Just as a car needs gasoline to run, your body needs fuel, too. Food is the fuel for your body. Food has calories, which are a form of energy. Your body burns this energy every day, and it uses even more when you exercise.

But you can't put just any fuel into your body. Your body needs certain types of food to keep it fit. You need carbohydrates, protein, fat, and water.

Carbohydrates are found in grains, such as bread, rice, and

pasta, and in fruits. You can find protein in beans, nuts, meat, fish, and in cheese and other dairy products.

You do need some fat in your diet. It helps your body absorb vitamins. But it's better to get fat from eating tuna than from eating french fries. Your body needs sugar, too, but it's better to get it from an apple than from a chocolate brownie. Fatty and sweet foods are OK for a treat once in a while. But it's better to fill up on foods that are healthy fuel.

Mix It Up!

A mix of foods is best, because your body needs something different from each one. No one food has everything your body needs to stay healthy. And remember to drink plenty of water!

Properly Equipped

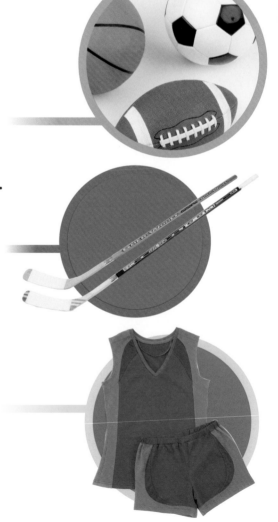

You'll need various equipment based on the type of activities you plan to do.

Gear: For many sports, you'll need a ball. Some balls are light and filled with air, like a kickball. Some balls are hard and solid, like a bowling ball. You may need to hit a ball. For tennis, you need a racket. For baseball, a bat. For hockey, you hit a puck with a stick.

Clothes: For all activities, you want to wear clothes that are comfortable and easy to move around in. Wear layers, so you can take a layer off if your body feels overheated.

Shoes: Sneakers are the best shoes for most activities. But you may need a shoe specifically designed for the sport you play, such as cleats for soccer or boots for skiing.

Safety: When you ride a bike, play football, or rock climb, you need a helmet to protect your head from injury. Some sports, such as racquetball, snowboarding, and swimming, require goggles to protect your eyes. You can protect your knees and elbows with pads when you in-line skate. Shin guards protect your legs in soccer.

Water: Your body is made mostly of water. When you are active, especially on hot days, you lose water when you sweat. You need to drink lots of water, even if you don't feel thirsty. You should drink before, during, and after physical activity.

Warm Up and Cool Down

Warming up is preparing your body to do exercise. When you warm up, your heart rate increases gradually. You're sending more blood to your muscles, so when you start to exercise, they are ready to go.

To warm up, do the activity you plan to do, just a little slower, for about five to 10 minutes. Walking is a good way to warm up before running. Bike slowly on a flat surface before you start biking fast or up hills. Jumping jacks get your whole body moving.

Don't stretch to warm up. You should never stretch cold muscles. Wait until you are warmed up, then stretch the muscles you plan to use.

When exercising, you shouldn't suddenly stop, especially if your

heart rate is still high. You need to cool down by doing a lighter exercise for about five to 10 minutes until your heart rate and breathing are back to normal again.

Walking is a great cool down for all types of exercise. You can also do some stretches. Stretch out the muscles that you used during your exercise to keep them from feeling sore later.

Sweat

Sweat is your body's natural way of cooling down. Sweat evaporates, and this takes the heat away from your body.

Outside Obstacle Course

An obstacle course is a challenging physical activity. It keeps your heart pumping as you hurry from one activity to the next. It also gives your muscles a workout.

Determine a starting line and a finish line. Decide on about five to seven activities, and set them up. You can do the obstacle course with two players racing at the same time, or let one person go at a time, record how fast he or she completes the course, and see if the next person can do it faster.

For two players racing at the same time, both wait at the start line. Someone says "Go!"

First stop: *Jump rope!* Jump rope for 10 jumps.

Next stop: *Hula hoops!* Step into a hula hoop laid on the ground. Lift it up over your head. Lay it down again, and repeat five times.

Next stop: *Hopscotch!* Hop across a hopscotch grid on the sidewalk.

Next stop: *Dribbling!* Dribble a soccer ball with your feet across a field, weaving between orange sport cones. If you miss a cone, you have to go back.

Last stop: *Sack race!* Step into a sack, grab the edges, and start hopping.

Cross the finish line and celebrate!

Tug-of-War

Tug-of-war is a strength game played with a group. The object is to see which team is stronger.

Find a flat area for your tug-of-war. Mark a line on the ground to be your center line.

Mark the rope in the center with a piece of colored tape. Measure an even distance from the center of the rope on both sides and mark with the colored tape. This will show how far each team needs to pull the rope across the line on the ground to win.

What You'll Need

- A judge
- An even number of people (from six to 20)
- A long, strong rope
- Colored tape

Divide the people into two even teams. The teams line up on opposite sides of the rope behind the tape markers. Some team members should stand on one side of the line and others should stand

on the opposite side. The strongest person should be at the end. He or she is called the anchor.

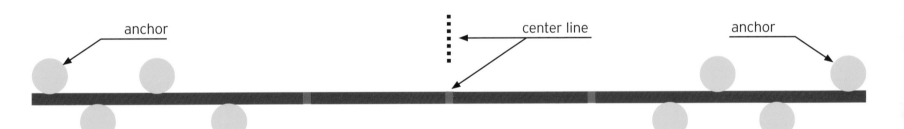

anchor

center line

anchor

When the judge says "ready," everyone lifts the rope. The judge makes sure the rope is pulled tight and that the center line on the rope is lined up with the center line on the ground. When the judge says "pull," everyone pulls.

Each team tries to keep its taped marker from crossing over the center line while trying to pull the other team's marker past the center.

On a Roll

If you're into wheeled sports, the possibilities are endless. You might ride a scooter or bike, glide on inline skates, or catch some air on a skateboard. And all these activities are fun whether you're alone or playing with friends.

If you want to add a little competition to your fun, set up a racecourse. Choose a starting line and a finish line. Set up orange sport cones between the two lines. Make sure there is enough room between cones for you to skate, bike, scoot, or skateboard

Safety First

Make sure to wear safety gear, especially if you're racing. If you fall, a helmet, knee pads, elbow pads, wrist guards, and gloves can help prevent injuries.

through. You can time yourself and try to better your time on each run. Or, if you're playing with friends, you can time one another and try to complete the course the fastest.

Square Dancing

Square dancing has a long tradition in American history. In addition to music, square dancing has a caller who calls out moves for the dancers.

Everyone finds a partner, and each couple gets in "home position" (right). The dancers make a square shape.

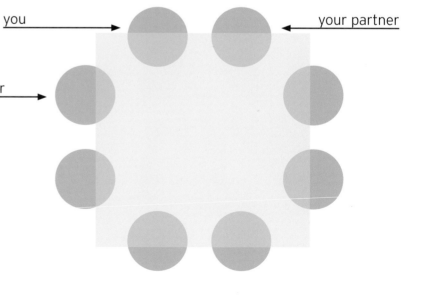

you

your partner

your corner

Then the caller starts calling out moves. Some common moves include:

Bow to your partner: Boys bend at the waist, and girls curtsy.

Bow to your corner: Your corner is the person next to you on your other side (not your partner).

Circle right or circle left: All dancers join hands and walk in a circle until they are back at their home position.

Promenade: You and your partner hold right hands and left hands, so that your hands are crossed in front of you. All the partners walk in a circle back to home.

Do-si-do: Face your partner, then walk past each other touching right shoulders. Stay facing the same direction as you move around your partner so that you are back to back, then walk backward past each other touching left shoulders until you return to your spot.

Right-hand or left-hand swing: Grab the right hand of your partner, as if you are shaking hands, switch places, and then switch again until you are back home. Then grab the left hand of your corner, and swing around each other until you are home again.

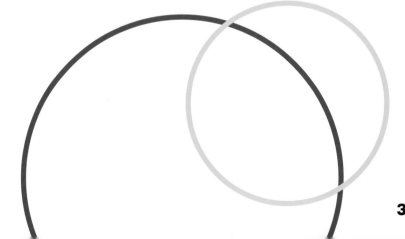

Yoga Poses

People have been practicing yoga in India for thousands of years. Through stretches and focus on breathing, yoga makes you more flexible and more relaxed.

In yoga, you pose your body in various ways. The poses are often named for elements of nature.

Cat pose

Get on all fours. Breathe in. As you breathe out, round your back up and drop your head.

- An exercise mat
- Comfortable clothes
- Water

Cat pose

Mountain pose

Stand with your legs and back straight and arms at your sides. Try to stand as tall and still as a mountain.

Tree pose

Stand straight. Slowly raise your right foot and press the bottom flat against the inside of your left leg. Then stretch your arms up to the sky like branches. Hold the pose, then try it with the other leg.

Cobra pose

Lie flat on your stomach. Place your hands flat on the mat even with your chest. Breathe out and lift your upper body off the mat as you straighten your arms. Look toward the sky.

Tree pose

Cobra pose

33

Triathletes

Some people like to swim. Some like to bike. Some like to run. A triathlete is a person who does all three.

Triathletes compete in triathlons, which combine swimming, biking, and running races into one event. The shortest triathlons are called sprints. They include swimming up to 0.6 mile (1 kilometer), biking up to 15.5 miles (25 km), and running up to 3 miles (5 km). The longest triathlons are

called Ironman triathlons —a 2.4-mile (3.8-km) swim, a 112-mile (180-km) bike, and a 26.2-mile (42-km) run. Thousands of people all over the world compete in these ultimate races.

Among the most challenging parts of triathlons are the transitions. The swimmers come out of the water, put on shoes and helmets, and hop onto their bikes. After the bike race, they stop to take off their helmets and may change shoes and other clothes before they start to run.

Longer triathlons may take all day to finish. The athletes have no time to stop, so they need to refuel their bodies as they race. Volunteers hand out water and sports drinks along the way, and competitors snack on energy bars or gels while they race.

Wheelchair Sports

Wheelchairs help people who cannot walk. But wheelchairs don't keep people from playing sports and staying fit.

Wheelchair basketball is a popular sport. It began in the 1940s. Many soldiers came home from World War II unable to use their legs. They became wheelchair users, and they needed a way to exercise. Teams formed at veterans' hospitals across the United States. They started touring

An athlete competed in a race in the Paralympic Games.

to compete with one another. Soon men in wheelchairs formed the National Wheelchair Basketball Association (NWBA). Women's teams also formed.

Much of the world got involved. Teams formed in other countries, and wheelchair basketball became an international sport. They held championships and also became a part of the Paralympic Games—an Olympics designed for people with disabilities. In addition to wheelchair basketball, the Paralympic Games includes events such as wheelchair curling, fencing, rugby, and tennis.

Lots to Do!

Many sports have been adapted for people with disabilities. Horseback riding, skiing, biking, water skiing, sailing, kayaking, archery, tennis, and bowling are all enjoyed.

Fit for a Cause

Staying fit doesn't just get you healthy. It can help others, too. Many towns and groups sponsor races and events to raise money to help those in need.

The American Heart Association sponsors Jump Rope for Heart each year for kids in elementary school. Children raise money by asking friends and family for donations. A donation may be a set amount, or a person can pledge a certain amount for each minute the child jumps rope. Then the kids jump rope in their schools. The money they raise supports research to solve many heart-related problems.

Race for the Cure is a 3-mile (5-km) race and fitness walk held all over the United States. The money raised by the millions of participants helps with efforts to find a cure for breast cancer.

Even kids can come up with ways to stay fit and help others at the same time. When Shawna Bush was an eighth-grader in Burlington, Connecticut, she decided to help her young neighbor Carter Shingleton. He has Prader-Willi syndrome, a complex genetic disorder. Shawna wanted to raise money to help find a cure. She held a walk-a-thon and invited friends, neighbors, and family. On a humid Saturday, more than 50 people gathered at the local high school to do laps on the track. Shawna raised $2,500 to help Carter, and at the same time helped everyone there get fit.

Carter Shingleton and Shawna Bush

Everyone, Everywhere, Every Day

Kids all over the world love to play, and playing is the best way to get fit. Just sitting to play video games doesn't count. You need to be up and active. Kickball, jumping rope, and even juggling count as physical activity.

Every day can be a "fit" day. You can take the stairs instead of an elevator. You can walk the dog or climb a tree. Towns have teams and classes. Sign up! You can play football, baseball, or soccer. You can take dancing, karate, or gymnastics classes.

Get active in the water. You can go canoeing, swimming, or surfing. Play in the snow. You can ski, ice skate, or sled. Be active on your own by taking a bike ride around your block. Be active with your family by going on a nature hike.

Set a physical activity goal you can achieve. "I want to be the fastest kid in school" is probably an unrealistic goal. No matter how hard you try, you may never reach it. "I want to be able to run a mile in 10 minutes or less" is better. Train your body by running a little farther or faster each day. Then you can reach your goal.

What Happened When?

5000 B.C.	800 B.C.	500 B.C.	1700	1800	1900

500 B.C. The Persian Empire reaches its height, and its warriors undergo strict fitness training.

1936 Jack LaLanne, a fitness expert, opens his first "health studio" where people can come to exercise.

776 B.C. The first Olympic Games are held in Olympia, Greece.

1700 Gymnastics becomes a popular way to stay fit in Germany, Great Britain, and the Scandinavian countries.

5000 B.C. Yoga begins in India.

1896 The modern Olympic Games are held in Athens, Greece.

1960 **1970** **1980** **1990** **2000** **2010**

1978 The first Ironman triathlon is held in Hawaii.

2008 At the Olympics in Beijing, China, American athlete Michael Phelps wins eight gold medals, an Olympic record.

1966 President Lyndon Johnson starts the Presidential Physical Fitness Award Program (now called the President's Challenge).

1999 Hicham El Guerrouj of Morocco breaks the record for the world's fastest mile, running it in 3 minutes and 43 seconds.

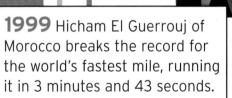

1996 The first U.S. surgeon general's report on physical activity and health is released.

Fun Fitness Facts

Wheelchair racers can be seen at almost any marathon. These athletes use specially designed hand-powered wheelchairs.

Ancient Greek Olympians did not win medals. They were presented with wreaths of olive branches to wear on their heads.

Your body has more than 650 muscles.

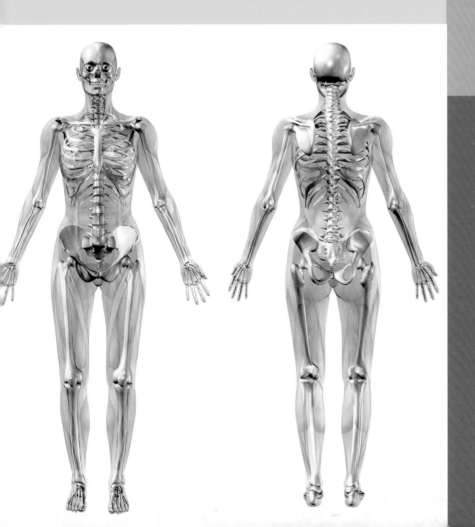

You have 62,500 miles (100,000 km) of blood vessels in your body.

Only men could compete in the ancient Olympics. But Kyniska, the daughter of a Spartan king, ignored the rules and competed in the chariot races in 396 and 392 B.C. She was the driver—it was the owner of the horse who got to wear the victory wreath.

Fitness Words to Know

aerobic exercises: exercises that strengthen your heart so it can better deliver oxygen and nutrients to your body

circulatory system: system in charge of delivering blood to all parts of your body

cooling down: recovering after exercise by gradually decreasing your heart rate

fitness: keeping your body healthy

flexibility: ability to easily move your muscles and joints

heart rate: how many times your heart beats in a minute

joint: where two bones meet and move

physical education: classes that teach you how to be fit

repetition: one of a series of repeated exercises

respiratory system: body system in charge of taking in and letting out air

skeletal muscles: muscles attached to your bones that help you move

strength exercises: exercises that focus on making individual muscles or muscle groups stronger

transitions: times between events in a triathlon when racers change equipment and clothes

triathlete: someone who competes in swimming, biking, and running races

warming up: preparing your body to exercise by gradually increasing your heart rate

yoga: stretching exercises that make you more flexible and relaxed

Other Words to Know

carbohydrates: substances your body needs that are found in grain and fruit

contract: to get shorter

endorphins: chemicals in your brain linked to happiness

evaporate: to enter the air

Prader-Willi syndrome: genetic disorder that affects many of the body's functions

protein: substance your body needs that is found in meat, beans, nuts, and dairy products

tension: slight pull

Where to Learn More

MORE BOOKS TO READ

Goulding, Sylvia. *Keeping Fit*. Vero Beach, Fla.: Rourke Publishing, 2005.

Miller, Edward. *The Monster Health Book: A Guide to Eating Healthy, Being Active & Feeling Great for Monsters & Kids!* New York: Holiday House, 2006.

Rockwell, Lizzy. *The Busy Body Book: A Kid's Guide to Fitness*. New York: Crown Books for Young Readers, 2004.

ON THE ROAD

The Basketball Hall of Fame
1000 W. Columbus Ave.
Springfield, MA 01105
877/446-6752

National Baseball Hall of Fame and Museum
25 Main St.
Cooperstown, NY 13326
888/425-5633

ON THE WEB

For more information on this topic, use FactHound.

1. Go to *www.facthound.com*

2. Choose your grade level.

3. Begin your search.

This book's ID number is 9780756540319

FactHound will find the best sites for you.

INDEX

ABOUT THE AUTHOR

Dana Meachen Rau has written more than 200 books for children, both fiction and nonfiction. When she is not writing books, she tries to stay fit. She loves riding her bike in the summer, cross-country skiing in the winter, and playing outside all year long with her family in Burlington, Connecticut.